Free Verse Editions

Edited by Jon Thompson

EMPIRE

Tracy Zeman

Winner of the New Measure Poetry Prize

Parlor Press
Anderson, South Carolina
www.parlorpress.com

Parlor Press LLC, Anderson, South Carolina, 29621

Printed in the United States of America
S A N: 2 5 4 - 8 8 7 9

Library of Congress Cataloging-in-Publication Data on File

978-1-64317-118-0 (paperback)
978-1-64317-119-7 (PDF)
978-1-64317-120-3 (ePub)

1 2 3 4 5

Cover design by David Blakesley
Cover art by Sarah Nesbit. Used by permission.

Parlor Press, LLC is an independent publisher of scholarly and trade titles in print and multimedia formats. This book is available in paperback and ebook formats from Parlor Press on the World Wide Web at http://www.parlorpress.com or through online and brick-and-mortar bookstores. For submission information or to find out about Parlor Press publications, write to Parlor Press, 3015 Brackenberry Drive, Anderson, South Carolina, 29621, or email editor@parlorpress.com.

Contents

Grass for Bone *5*

    Grass for Bone *7*

    The Edge Effect *21*

    Solitary Branches & Small Leaves *22*

Star or Plow *27*

    Star or Plow *29*

    Outliers & Blueprints *34*

    Broad Wings above Tall Grass *35*

    Simulacra *36*

    Large Stone on Body, Birch Branches Above *41*

    Pope County, Illinois *42*

    Plum Blossoms at Yellow Dusk *45*

Empire of Grass *51*

    Grist *53*

    Taxonomic *54*

    Midewin *64*

    Empire of Grass *65*

Notes *69*

Acknowledgments *71*

About the Author *73*

Free Verse Editions *75*

For Edward Zeman, 1951-2004

Empire

And the grease of the engine itself
At the extremes of reality
Which was not what we wanted

—George Oppen

Thou little spade of mine
Leaving nooks for Daisy
And for Columbine

—Emily Dickinson

Grass for Bone

Grass for Bone

Small cakes of lily-seed   an assembly
of swallows branch-bound   assembly of
clouds burst   your face washed
in pigment   no *sati* under pitch
under night & timber heat
skin burnt to blister   living into
atrophy or *enclave*   the mouth of a horse
tells the beginnings of the age
of grass   of red spearfish shale & black hills
a reconstructing reckless this getting
& becoming lost   you the figure
of crouched skeleton under gaze
how bounded the boundless
new area of contestation

*

Red crowned field sparrow
trills in minor-key in minor places
cut forests now shrubland of
fences & abandoned pastures
sieve of redbud leaves sewn together
like a length of rope   engineer a noose
pink-billed new-world   song plaintive
& unceasing during the search for another
noise herded into rows & hoof-prints
where old railway decays into foxglove
stream carves into gully   into dusk into
bodies boiled in lye then scraped clean
turning bones into rusted machinery
a stand of pale orchids no longer

*

A tomb constructed of bark   this remainder
covered with branches with lichen & rock
painted yellow & decorated with feathers
contains three figures of straw & one man
arms tied with a thin sheet of wood
a still creek flat & frozen
corpse placed with head sunward
the direction of origin of ancestor
miles & miles & miles & miles
life that we called *yours* on a good day
on a good day this love for you
a "house of wooden fingers"
house wren in a tree hollow
tree hollow occupied with bone & straw

*

Two rivers "ticking softly into one"
leaf-cutter chronicle   a fern frond left
in a bath of sedges & blackbirds
our "machine in the garden" over &
over   slash of green   sweep of
gray   thought beneath so slight
a field of white-lipped peccaries
under the piha's ascending whistles
& screams   the chronicler   the echo-
maker   "we must not worry
how few we are & fall from each
other"   a boat-like shape in the dark
of the milky way   a way of knowing
brings the world forth as not

*

Trade horse for tea & tea for horse
this cobblestoned knowing brings us
into being   we must worry we must
a clutch of red & cream white eggs
silly goose   mud-caked & barefoot
among dry sticks trash & moss
an occasional sentinel   how to occupy this
desert world   our little camp
our little home inside where a lamp burns
uncertainly yellow then white then
wild plum or peach leaf willow & smartweed
we feed our horses with cottonwood
upon this spotted plain
an open grove   a glitter of flint

*

Arabian ostrich   Atitlán grebe
black-faced honeycreeper endemic &
no more   our trail canopied in wild
grape & sunflowers   did I say *counterfeit*
or *crabapple   coneflower* or *copy*
prairie after heavy rain will soak
a man on horseback up to his waist
water clinging to bluestem
grass clinging to wind & sun
an ache in the bone a litany in negative
we stand at the river's edge to watch
the fish swallow what's left
of you   this *keno* a bathing place
for the after   & the rest also

*

12

Red buffalo pushes the hardwood east
trees & wheat & dust
an ache in the rind   after a summer storm we are
without the way   defined by absence by
presence of great feats   a morass this
place of ours   fire licked grasses & rushes
define the treeline we share
with the rest   carrion cardinal compass-flower
bringing a way of being with
not against   into rivers oceans empty
into oceans rivers splinter   a continuum
that sparks this consolation of *sow*
& *form* of *joint* & *oxbow*   you empty
into this & splinter into that

*

"To wander in restless want & penury"
to wear a necklace of green herbs
to keen over the corpse embalmed
with honey & washed in water of chamomile
of blackened faces for thirty days
of water poured on the roots of the nearest tree
of *feasting* & *footbridge* of being sewn in
a mat of threadbare linen   day at its most
long   its most blue   sky knit with clouds
mountains crowded with long-needled pines
lying flat & still   on a good day this love
stopped with cloth & cardamom
a plumed chimney reduces the muscles
to ash   a fern in a summer fire

*

A wire cage of fledglings   bluish-white eggs
of the California condor   yellow-faced then
red   extant & permeable   a "member of
the cloud" & cliff   the boundary between this
world & that thought to be impermanent
at times   grasses grow in the rain
shadow of the Rockies   islands in a sea of steppe
a tract for dying a good death   or dying well
anoint with the right thumb   eyelids ear lobes & lips
ovenbird catbird warbler wren
what of the marker between
the human & all else   misplace a howling
experience   skins drying over coals
smoke broken into silos & rings

*

Mountain as adaptation   quick clouds
rags of mist   wolf elk bison bear
creatures of grass plains & burrow
contained a skull wrapped in woven cotton
ancestor figure fashioned of wood & mud
of one shepherd or another   principle of
center of dislodging to introduce other
order   old skin over this
truth as bald as cold as middle
no meddle   every settlement had a house
set apart for the dead   new way of burial
as manipulation as a tactic for conversion
funeral as cover for war   "a month's mind"
untenable   the red deer the cordgrass

*

Summit or *sun*   living rock
to which the heart is given   by obsidian
skeletons disarticulated & tied into bundles
before the ossuary   furthest part of the world
must be *sunset* & *sea*   moldering   the order upset
loggerhead shrike   peregrine falcon
black-footed ferret   the Missouri River hems
the Big Horn Mountains   a hinge between
one land & another   an effigy was made
of wood & wax   verisimilitude will have to suffice
for aspen for sage-thrasher for pipit
stalks burnt like feathers   convoy of
corn & flesh   hope to graft the present to
the predicament   to all my tenderness

*

Canary's corpse   copse of false
Solomon's seal   rivets of stars & sharp notes
the men were "found slain
with their mouths stopped full of bread"
beneath the blue lupine & wild strawberry
by springtime only a hundred were left
having subsisted on dogs cats rats & mice
gust goes   obscured by the storm   entrust
hope inherent & lashed   tincture of snow
some shrieking   O & you no longer
named what you were   a handful
of farm buildings behind the windbreak
wheat planted in alternating fallow strips
how the cinder draped the field then

*

Wasp's nest found inside a skull
the tiny clay pot of the mud dauber
dispossessed island   of trees & people
wilderness makes it hard to be
"unregarded & unburied"
bodies decaying in the hedgerows
after surviving on only oysters for eight weeks
ineffable slight   the land not an after
thought   ember or tinder   particular disaster
headed for half-lives   for we are tied
to the place that made us   no ledger
for that map   mouse-nest   eggshell
slaughter   cellar   sequester   root out
what as remedy for this condition

*

Vanilla grass & sage brush flank the hills
a gleaner   an ax an owl a honeycomb
knee-deep leaf-rot   a certain joylessness
a cage of ribs   apple trees leafing on a slope
a chance to still the worst of it
wreck of thaw   encampment of charred wood
pheasant quail hare   what of plenty
of mending or maelstrom   private burials
disallowed for fear of covering up
the "violent context of life"
flocks of cranes landing on a bank
filament fissure sawgrass
surely we'll survive if apprehensive
if fixing the outside within the frame

The Edge Effect

Dead end path through woods
in spring thaw   prairie grouse stomps
          & booms on the lek
pinnated subterfuge   "repairs to a torn fabric"
draglines & clay-tiles in April break
into lonely wild sounds   two orange pockets
appear & disappear in feathers
on pre-dawn hilltop   a sun a sail a shoot

"Each life conveys to some certain center"
she said   a cracked canoe on the riverbank
bleak iron-hard & white   lifeless & unknit
meadow voles tear up a newly disked field
          with their tiny crooked furrows
if lake torn from rock   if *war* in *warrant*
in *warbler*   in *warm* & *wary*   later in summer
monarchs float above milkweed

Chipping sparrow feeds a fledgling
throat to throat   grit-heartbeat
dreaming sometimes of one thing or another
burned warrior on pavement
                    a grasshopper clicking
a shovelnose sturgeon making its way
from the Missouri to the Mississippi
silt-fast   lock-slow   silver-blue

Solitary Branches & Small Leaves

Barnloft odor of bedstraw & dust
tiny ripples in a system of decay
dogs chase a deer across the field
"land without bottom or edge"
bird with light set against backdrop
unlike *sunrise* or *moonglow*   roving winter-
wren in the weeds   abbreviated tail

High-pitched song   obfuscated reportage
slowly becomes master of everything
that loneliness   a part with power
to suggest a whole   traces of red paint
on the door   attribute high mortality rates
to depravity   to roam to be the by-product
of progress   salt-lick herd of elk or deer

Traps set on headwaters & animal wallows
a sora-rail's black face on gray salt marsh
an otter swimming in the river at dusk
head skimming the water's surface
"loveless & sleepless the sea" I said
"a human problem" I said   "the red flag
is black to the bull" but not to us

*

Some kind of mistake
to buy an empire with beads & cloth
he was scored across both cheeks
face   hands   legs   back
left a tolerably good horse on the shoal
the wave's force determines the pebbles' size
red as rule   starlight fox coralberry

To cut a piece from the soil
of a failed state   panic had seized the men
like wild fire   like fire to cut a piece
from a heart heavily burdened
build bulwark next time   shoreface
lagoon   Little Flat Lick   hills & the new
broken into pieces into self heart bird

Mutable & unfit   so the story goes
to pare down   mountain-mallow
stickseed   pondberry   "species
are unfixed" he said   this greenwashing
once was rock-right   barefoot
& lake & cliffs hanging over
a sea   de-wilded   badger at the center

*

Rain fell intermittently   fiercely
"the dead boy was found clasping a tree"
his wounds had been dressed
with elm bark   no honeyed words
only ill-starred & reduced
turkeys dropt dead off their roosts
hogs frozen to death in their pens

A rope knotted red   ideas of first
& second at odds again
"your love will be safe with me"
I said   red-hearted on the overgrown path
it's important to forget while constructing
a nation   a hybrid space
a man dead in the road left

For some days   failed to recognize new
paradigm   "drunk on the sale
the scale of the natural world"
a gull trying to swallow a starfish whole
a yellow-rumped warbler at Lost Lake
"a woman hid in a hollow
gave birth to a child during the night"

*

No stars yet only frogs croaking
wind in trees   waves in wind
"did not man maim by no" belief
in alterity   delicacy in skin
all else is packhorse & stolen boots
in hard rain & hierarchies
the ocean at night looks like sky

"A grave between the rocks"
a "bodiless campaign" turning soil
to stone   a black gorge   a guidepost
a carapace aglow in darkness
"stayed by the dead hand of inaction"
of star-gazer culler boarder
shipwrecked upon the idea of unwilled

"In the forests maple trees cracked
like pistols & burst open with frozen sap"
I thought of you & where you'd gone
a great destiny   some leave-taking
carried in pieces over the rugged hills
mudholes big-sloughs bare-legged
every few yards some body growing without

Star or Plow

Star or Plow

Inside the longhouse the dead are arranged
according to rank   corrupt bodies
shrouded in animal skins
dog teeth   potsherds   cut wood
stacked along the outer walls
as women collect the bones of their kin

For the charnel house   bows arrows tobacco
a bear paw   a turtle effigy pipe
a fledged sparrow rubbing its neck
on a hackberry branch   a mask of seashells
finding its way west by trade
a buffalo jump   a new blind flood

Shattering the Clovis & leaving a mark
in the black mat running through layers of strata
after water filled the land
horse   camel   dire wolf   *bison antiquus*
extinct or expatriated   "that phraseless melody"
perhaps in the rediscovery one *you* will be found

One "shiverer round the door"

*

Unearthed in the black court
that line in the rock for *ice* & *empty*
for *star* then *plow*   the sure-to-come
is never close enough
to unsettle the edge of the human landscape
a narrow tract of grass along the highway

Black-eyed Susans blazing stars
& cattails in the medians   along the railroad
a biologist discovers a rare wingless grasshopper
keyacris scurra in the kangaroo grass
Jefferson's enumerators sent west to populate
his drawing room   his science of specimen & capture

Of geometry democracy steel steam
seed & theft   for the good of us all
for the good of shining persons
with hearts all one stone   a country bird
heels to law & need   a country boy
locks the plains in a grid

We are all freeholders still

*

This alienated posture   we went out upon
the world as   "went out
upon circumference"   to fix a flux inside
the rain   a rain that follows the plow
as it drifts & divides
to gain a foothold against a ghost

As if air could be netted
"sturdy little countenance against the wind"
fifty million bison now
forty-five million cattle   an outline for our eventual
inability to escape from circumstances
home implies a border implies

The mountain plover a ground feeder
the burrowing owl occupying a prairie dog's nest
to roam is not to be without
form but rather to be formed in serial
unsluiced from a territorial tyranny
stands of blue bunch wheat grass & willows

Unlining a creek bed sunken silted & fast

*

To sluice or still a creek with cattle
carcasses   in winter a wintry condition
moves steadily down "the dream
of civilizing a wilderness"   more than half the range
had lost more than half   degraded by grazing
the riparian the headland the hill

How could imagining lead to obsolescence
a wayfarer   the root's white foot a force
under snow or fire   increasers & decreasers
hay-balers barbed wire & antibiotics
this underpinning   "a postponeless creature"
no darker despot so restful in the enclosure

The enclosed constructions of the present
become hard to recognize as home
for bluebird for Henslow's sparrow for bobolink
these fields without fencerow
or windbreak   new oligarchy
"the sound of the prairie being plowed

Was that of a fusillade of pistols"

*

Knowledge as the composition of a body
subsoil   aquifer   trail of thorn & thistle
at any given moment   divisible
savage   nomad   disciples when the west was
abundant in fescue bunchgrass & light
unbent   "if what we could—

Were what we would"   cessation implies
succession   sediment ash dust sand
seed   a borrowed dwelling   itself an echo
yourself   displaced   envy what is already
false or scarce   "the color of the grave
is green"   "the color of the grave is white"

Is reprieve to replace us   no employment here
in this weedy plutocracy of parceled plots
with no way to overcome
enough   life as almost straight
as most unlike   a snowbound hill   an elk
in a winter range   a blight of dry lightning

Mountain scissoring a big sky over grass

Outliers & Blueprints

August finch drowned in a barrel of rain
heat-choked grass fills a field
in late-summer   "common tongue
of veneration"   copper kettles
& iron knives   a barefoot collection
of shorebirds & blueprints

      Blue springs & blue estuaries
moon-surge pale-grey above backyard
practice of abet & accord   rain-drenched
cardinal *chip chips* weatherblind
on the wire   unencumbered
red-crested acumen

*

      "Necklace of shell beads"
a crowd of curlews feeding on a tidal flat
prairie passage   partridge pea flowering
alley-side   opossum night-feasting
in the compost piled high   excavate
pit & cob   standing at the edge

        Of some cavity
waiting to toss the bones under
a *clearing-house*   a *palisade*
earth augmented with tree roots & landmarks
"carefully washed dressed & ritually fed"
the *snap snap* of prairie shoestring

Broad Wings above Tall Grass

We watch bank swallows
flitter out from a cliff face   hunting mayflies
on the wing   hikers mistake them for midday
bats   water pools below & castoff branches
                    swim in runoff & moss

Crowding of ditch & field from row crops
hedge-apple smashed roadside
its white seedy heart exposed   a white-tailed deer
stiff eyeless & blank lay gutted
                    in gravel & mud   possess

Principle pilgrim   a circular bricked barn
decaying windmill   pasture thistle &
marsh-marigold   fleabane   streams & rivers
high after heavy June rains   run thick & brown
                    to cut one's teeth on comfort

        On creature   a dark speck in the updraft
smattering of species   swirling mass
of redtails & Swainson's hawks   after wintering
on grasshoppers   nest on low rimrock ledges
                    clutches of two or three

Salt Creek feeds the Sangamon in a straight line
its former course   a checkered-skipper oscillating
among hollyhocks & poppies   we climb the little hill
loess light under our feet   a soft summer
            a horse a few hands on the common good

Simulacra

Tree-trunks buttressed against wind
& seasons of rain   crested chickadee
peeto-s from redbud branches   a tangle
of tea leaves in a yellow gaiwan
edged with cranes   hailstone
honey bee   the wren's cocked tail
a wilderness of reserves & timber leases
refuge of frost & stars   of fire & sumac
stands of prickly pear   a bluff against
a floodplain where the Spoon River meets
the Illinois   wood thrush   larkspur
sugar pine   ruby-throated hummingbird
a measured meadow   a shifting resembling
something human rather than world
a moveable plethora   the bank littered
with small hills of bone   canopies of
bear-skins & branches   eight spear-heads
within a mammoth rib-cage

*

Beneath pressed earth   a locust
horse bones   an enemy whose lips have been
sawed off   the white of two moths
a second as a killing thing   chipped flint
dolmen   stone table   an economy
of placelessness   stone as the skeleton
of this   casualties of dwelling
light tree darkness seed   midnight barred
owl in a hemlock tree   columbine sprouting
from rock interpolated in the cliff's face
muffled vastness   marauders traveling
towards a time of no & nothing
of heat & crowding   a word a presence deferred
like any to conceal   a waterjar a white-throated
sparrow   dead wood mistaken
for bone for wellworn for a culture that will
replace even its originator & the land
becomes common & again

*

A cardinal's red fray   as he circles
on the line   a ruby-crowned kinglet
in October migration   flitting white then
gold   does pilgrim mean without
place or progress   a bison trail for railroad
slate-colored junco for windrow
of dead trees   a crown a bower   to carry
away the world   the old seabed that is
now the Great Plains   "he told me
death was dead"   "many a bitterness—had
been—"   the bobwhite's once familiar
call   "a vast zero" a sound a weed
a record of malice   dawn drawn down by
a zest for one kind of living & not
another   15,000 bodies buried in a rocky ravine
land *of little use* to most   goes
unnoticed for 200 years   scrap
scarp   twilight   forge & plot

*

Dark spread on sound   rocks shells
broken plates   wine bottles   some sound spread
on dark   here lies the wild sea   here lies
a greened gap   a syllable for *neck* for *chest*
for *spring*   some stones depicted a hand
cutting down a tree   some carved
sandstone into figure of neck & head   here
lies a boy in a tree   a blank & unfocused thing
some "familiar species that perished
by the door"   gathering wood & consoling
themselves   buried outside the walls
with "eyes that looked on wastes"
& a "blank—& steady wilderness"
a litter of bean poles wrapped
in thin bark for carrying away corpses
& the wounded   this dead man this pale
wood   this black horse
a lead horse   a hearse for now

*

To see dimly is to see
the ground covered in beads   tawny & loosed
in sandreed bottlebrush & sage smudge
ground-cherry horned-lark nightfall
want   a shell a boy inside stopless
a body a heavy white frost   "the red—
blaze" of the morning undreamt—
a ceremony underpins it   rocks ice
water air   to distinguish a certain
shatter   for certain this nutshell   goatgrass
a bull elk's bugle in fall rut
French's shooting-star at Lusk Creek
that a self is the extension of all these
a midland of hickory & oak   a flock
of coreopsis   black walnut & sugar maple
rawboned   airy   fine   how far
are you from *aslant* or *asunder*   rain
on dry leaves   on unable & undone

Large Stone on Body, Birch Branches Above

Arriving by flatboat by upland plain
as the Ohio empties into the Illinois
the sweet singer whistles
his *peabody* song   his "heart of hay"
of heath aster   of the meadowlark's black bib

Often flesh often keep-sake often scrap
of key or spoon or coin buried
on a ridge   a white-footed mouse
in a woodcock's nest   blue grama swaying
on the split slope steppe

Carved stone positioned near a road
marks marsh   border   lake   & the driest hills
"we for ourselves" they thought   or last snow
of the season   try to make permanent
what was   yellow flax so lovely in spring

Pope County, Illinois

Cattle bones   baskets of soil & chalk
labor sedimented in land
junco on a bur oak
snow-covered   iron teeth dragged
over plowed field

      IDA HAZEL
      WA ᘔ BORNAPR
      IL ETHE30TH
      1787ANDDIEDJ
      ULYTHE14TH
          1810

Millstone Bluff   keyless split expel
blind   wind blowing   slashing
her north-facing stone   brown-
grey of winter forest frost
ravine with limestone bedrock
uninscribed footstone   a hairpin
"I was used—to the birds—
before—"

Before I was used to deadfall
on the Cumberland River
squatted acres   a singletree a kettle
rough stone gives dark
plied wood gives light   in dark
two horses   a house on water
unshaped creek & field stones

     PRINCESTHE
     CLAY MUST BE
     YOUR BED IN SPITE
     DEATH YOUR TOWARS
     THE TOAL PHE WISE
     THE REVERENT HED
     MUST LAY AS LOW AS
     OURS

A housewright   a bluejay bobbing as he
shrieks   black-beaked white-throated
this clay must be   holes instead
wing for eye   the river's horseshoe
"I have eaten it away"   as if
"like chaos—stopless—cool—"

Saline mines at Cave-in-Rock
after he purchased a single saddle
a resettling   a widow left with $38
a horse   11 hogs   a cow & calf
fit this vocation   this conviction
sawmill on top of the hill   the Great
Road   guess nothing   give dark

       R E M B E R M A N
       AS YOU PAS BY AS
       YOU AR NOW SO WONS
       WASI   YOU
       SOON MUST BE PR
       EPARE FOR DETH AND
       FOLLOW ME

           HEARE LIES
       THE BODDEY O

For several days in going
to field   a pair of
drawing chains   "the hemlock
likes to stand"   the whip-poor-will's whistle
this bed of birchbark & cotton grass

Plum Blossoms at Yellow Dusk

Unending rain-cloud   destruction
of reminders   *ton ho* or *the sweeping*
away of deer blind or fruit tree
panic-grass wild-rye goldenrod
here lies an amber bead   a regime
of lowlands & clay-pan   a few unburnt bones
& at the bottom of this stone upon
stone   the cutter   the polisher

The wilderness road   a blacktide
not something imagined but the most certain
of all false starts   only moon only cloud
only the great-horned owl at night
with white-bib & plumicorns
the conditions for the human argument
set against purple milkweed
& chickadees moving in pairs & you not

A few inalterable laws   rain on trillium
on spruce & rose-breasted grosbeak
defined in tandem   with social
constructions & displacements
the tune of two recorders nearby &
rock   tree   burial   she said
"for wilderness to exist
the landscape first had to be eradicated"

*

I told you what might have been lost
is lost   how persistently work makes world
work makes wild   broken tooth
pear-hawthorne   beardtongue
repetition versus progress   a form of *cultivation*
the little *chup chup* of the varied thrush
these ends   implicate ironweed or
growth in the form of *colony* or

Conversion or "an omen in the bone"
or "nesting in this poem" is
some sad wrong   keeping cover
along the river valleys & tributaries
big bluestem blooms purple & gray
on sandhills   outbreaks of yellow fever
"to die from too much feeling"
a perverse existence   "a last gaze

Was a potent memory"   bodies made
unrecognizable "conveyed a powerful picture
of social disorder" of a race lost of bones buried
in sand   "earth belongs in usufruct
to the living" he said   "standing for conquest"
a framework where images of dying fueled
aggression & salvation   four large trees
iron-branded with initials

*

Wild turkeys & cornstalks in a deserted field
a sense of loss & gain at once
fish-flesh bear-oil   to root in rot
a wood keeping cover   an extra horse apiece
many streams trailed north
from the little Tennessee along the Appalachians
to the Great Lakes   a tiny green heart
wild currant & stargrass

Hail then rain then canebrake
she made a study of chained trees
then buried a copy of tree
of bird of a new system
that relinquishes the person
a winter wren trilling in the understory
a cormorant in a cliff   "to trace back
to the source of living"   make order

From bunchberry loosestrife water-hemlock
in May the low prairie swales
a veritable flower garden
"I have been a long time in this story
of land-sigh half-bends & song-crime"
a dream meadowsweet
the *coo-hoo* of the burrowing owl
a state of suspension   a key in a latch

*

Two gulls chase an eagle into the rock
their young caught in its mouth
a newborn left in a cradle of bark
"the linkage of place & person" unstable
in us   a moth in rain   errant seeker
oxeye   meadow-violet   rosinweed
pea-vines moving up the line
of rivers   reluctant & irregular   a body

Found floating   illness from sin
"the dream of mastery" of mineral fiber
muscle   our complex relationship to reason
& its corrupt imitations   human betterment
"red in tooth & claw"   bubbling out
from the foot of a crag
she went back "to find her trail
devoured by birds"   a corollary

Brutish & sovereign   a wagon road
a baby found in the ruins   its head broken
shiploads of redemptioners for settling
bury a note in the dirt to lay claim
"declaration as weapon"   the moon full
& beautiful over the night-water
"I measure every grief" I meet
in this broken unbroken place

*

Dust-conjecture   two bats weaving
through the pines   golden-crowned kinglet
hooded warbler in spring woods
northern saw-whet owl   for how long
a shattered sequence   thickets
& timber   streams & small hills
a break in the mountains
a boy caught in a fire

Alone without bread salt horse or dog
veins of living   no drop of my blood
runs in this ravine of oak elm poplar
chestnut   "residue as well as raw material"
cost of purpose   fringes of human
"the dream of naturalism" unreal   moonlit-
hike to bluff over estuary   "climate
of unsuspended suns—"   shifting

Repository of upended & us
how does dwelling only seem to create
loss & onslaught   storm & injury
tattered facts   tired barbarity
twisting through underbrush   over boulders
& ledges   a bison trail an old road
if "marginal & imagined"   brick-eyed presage
false-boneset's thick taproot

Empire of Grass

Grist

        A thumb of grass in the East
& fingers of timbered stream valleys west-bound
a cowbird rolls an egg from a dickcissel's nest
parasite   decoy   pond-bed stocked
with winter-whitened antlers   the stag's sharp feet
cut through ice-crust   in January

             Trap   margin   throat
some deeper wilderness cement affords
head chest boy   transformation of skin
to highway   cottontail mud tryst
buzzard   split slip   inside the red gloss
hum   conductivity   carcass   a grasshopper

Forced into a niche by a red-headed woodpecker
immobile alive & soon-to-be devoured
& reshaped into something soft & shattered
three bodies swimming in a quarry
in June   an osprey nest atop a telephone pole
                minnows swarming beneath

A clear surface against hard gray rock
rivers will work to return to their shape
after being steered straight   "economic
migrants"   corroded agents   weld
cheek to torn in mid-day singe
           a line of high cliffs a sail a shot

Taxonomic

Mountains purpling   lichens weathering rock
trenches filled with tree limbs   "cabins perched
like birds" among hill clefts   dispossessed
by which "nothing means something"
she said   "a living fossil"   horsetails
& goats-beard rooting among spruce
a flock of buzzards preening on sand   a point
where surplus meets absence   or rain
means branch against window
at night   coyote   fox   long-eared owl

*

"Name given is no name" at all
red-spotted garter snake   dusky salamander
"orphaned brigade"   *burgeon* or
bereft   icon as artifact   under cover
of daylight   the heath hen disappears
expatriated to a single island   had been
peasant food   or first Thanksgiving
1932 no wild ones left   daylight in the trees
a lifeboat   a "failure of geographic imagination"
a Stellar's jay nesting outside the door

*

Bewick's wren tree-climbing after rain
to make nothing come before or after
"a delicate combination of dominance
& necessity"   stark lineaments   such comfort
to live in such dissolution   spiny sun-star
undulating in the shallow water
bull-kelp   beach strawberry & crabshell
low-tide again   revolve evolve   plumb
myriad   note date   site of capture
range & nomenclature   if briar if barren

*

A shell buried in an alpine meadow
a dozen seals beached on Westwind Spit
in the bluff's brush golden-crowned
sparrows flit & whip   ordered
& static   before we knew little "links in her
great chain" could be broken   bent   rusted
weatherworn   eastern cougar
Merriam's elk   spectacled cormorant
a "collective destination"   a cloud forest
two worlds inhabiting one mountainside

*

Hermit thrush rustles the ferns   the deep cooing
of a band-tailed pigeon high in the firs
cabinets of wonder "darkinfested"   the black
& white of the great auk   commodified in life
& in death   ecologically naive   old bones
buried in saltpeter   sea urchin skeleton
in the beach wrack   "systems produce their own
contradictions" she said   this view of self
to fuse that which was never apart
shore as circumspective   as thinly-worn

*

A teahouse on a fault-line
a series of new seacoasts   of our own
making   red with impasse or is it
white with resentment   black with
expiration   a mastodon's eyetooth
unburied on the Hudson River bank
farmer-traded for a half-pint of rum
embodiment of *link* & *rupture*
"humanity is engaged on equal burial"
plentitude & balance only notions of

*

Our signature in everything   believed
massive bones belonged to ancestors
antediluvian   men lions hunters soldiers
constantly unfolding geological strata
in the struggle for existence   barn swallows
glide near the water's surface   rust-
bellied   in fifty years world went
from orderly & new to "incomprehensively
old" & in endless flux   muted wildness
caretaker   cultivator   curlew

*

Treefrog chorus on both sides of the pond
in darkness   "bone encrusted marl-pit"
fence-crosser   disaggregator   he said
hard to live overlaid with wounds
a deer trail after snowfall
"to change & glow & darken under it"
eastern meadowlark on a rail   branches
splintering as this ghost-world slips
into *quarry* & *utter* & *midnight*
a "hard clear image"   a burned-out stable

*

As if no hand behind the stilled world
only vanishing   veiled-rancor   the guar
the wild yak   the whooping crane
whose colonies learn migration routes
from machines   that they might winter &
survive   seasons as modern as
nightfall studded with waking   with mudstone
& gleaming   post-glacial lake hidden in woods
pygmy owl's short whistle fills the canopy
with chalk & clay   treefall & contour

*

A "wind-leaned chicken coop" in a dusty yard
a form of humanity grounded in
unhindered & unfathomable   a skinned colt
dismembered & scattered in trees   streams
gullies   vulture wolf opossum   recasting
soft boundaries   garner ambiguity
unwaywardly   violence as derivative of
civilization   as "ecological imperialism" as
last wild quagga shot in 1870   to be cut-off
from narrative of place & of other

*

Purple finch near land's edge   song-
sparrow streaked russet & white   contentious
among leaves & skies   replete with lost
monikers   trees black against starred brink
real & false both erased   bearded vulture
red feathered & black masked   mud-drenched
bone-breaker   "re-dreamed
& then dreamed again" a minor surplus
an offering at the house's four corners
an "omen-bird"   a beginning & ending

*

Convocation of moths on window   white-
winged & transparent   a bull's eye
painted on a bison   wide firmament blackened
with birds   itinerant clouds   flattened
plains   "we move & move to undo
some mistake"   I dreamed that you were
dead   only you didn't know & I couldn't
velvetleaf   lambs-quarter   structure
of resistance   cockroach   shark   coelacanth
ginkgo   horseshoe crab   ancient & extant

*

Grassland dunes dotted with Pitcher's thistle
spotted sandpiper bobs in the reeds
as we walk the rocky beach   a raccoon
digs crayfish from shore mud   to cover
one's feet with wet sand & pine needles
surrounded by frog chatter   remoteless
terminal   deculturated   least-bitterns
nesting among tule rushes   "engrossed to
absolute—with shining—& the sky—"
inexhaustibility   prairie-sea   a type of chaos

*

Tree stump as symbol for progress   for
predestination   a myth perpetuator   a redactor
key   anchor   snake   bird   blind-eyed
urgency   a brook trout in a cold creek
twisting downhill   water over rock
marsh-ferns over bank   vast flocks
of pigeons foraging beechnuts acorns
& juneberries   wandering wanderer
"pots of burning sulfur   pine-knot torches
long poles"   hogs devoured what remained

*

A little blank in the "certainties
of sun"   in darkness the ocean
a sound like a far-away storm   on my back
the stars   the law   an echo-landscape
a rough-skinned newt eating the eggs
of the Pacific treefrog   expulsion as
costume   custom as competition
human as less than human   a double bind
a gouged gorge   a vacant paddock in summer
an unthinking cacophony   a pact

*

Green "etched sharp" into the space
of things   agency or bliss or field mouse
three blackbirds cackling in a forked tree
a carved figure leans against the crook
wet & dark from near-constant rain
the last of something   named "Martha"
dies September 1st 1914   rock-slumber
a trophy   a bleached skeleton
a teeming mass   a cloudgap
conflicting desires of *collect* & *conserve*

*

A clay heart   "a low dome of hills
as unknown as the river"   we traveled
through the backcountry   fish gun emptiness
the sound of not wood   day deadened
an afternoon moon overhead   we kill one
so that another may be controlled
"this daring & not daring"   this plain heart
railroad   salt   "blinded stool pigeons dropped
from platforms to lure"   trap or shoot
unparalleled satiation   premise & practice

*

To become the sole survivor   quiet
morning   a banana slug on my trail
biotic baseline   kingfisher hovering
above the Salmon River   tea leftover
from last night   a corrected story
some "rhetorical slippage"   driven to the sea
row upon row of coyote skins hung
on a rack   master of this   co-laborer
of a kind of "cultural harvest"   an osprey
floating over Cascade Head's three rocks

*

Horse & rifle & glut   two ring-necked
ducks drifting near the bridge   pale-cheeked
& dark-trimmed   along the rocky outcrops
"as many as 400 shooters" vying at once
parcels of animals "left to rot
where they fell"   leaving a foul odor
hanging in the air   refugees & vagrants
"of being is a bird" she said   or a butterfly
the silverspot & its coastal grasslands
its early blue violet & forest fringe

*

Olive-sided flycatcher stock-still
atop a dead silver fir in the sedge dunes
a juggernaut   a stronghold   a crescent
in the ridge   stake-out hawk & owl
flyways   see faint stars through cloud-cover
offer bounty for vermin & ravenous   for
nearness   akin to memory & to loss
to transgressing & wishbone   no place
to return to   only some composite-present
& I know it well & the clover & you

Midewin

        Two yellow eyes & a ringed tail at night
light wound through a key-hole   a skein
of oak-litter underfoot   animal body
among seed-pods & vines
              a knife   a row   a fence-line

Snaking its way through grass wedded
to wind   indigo bunting & kingbird
cottonwood stacked & railroad ties
uprooted between sod-covered bunkers   a herd
              of meadow-mounds   arsenal of

Red-winged blackbirds   flaw tarmac marsh
a trooped trope   unburdened
        openness with steely clatter   hill crowned
by prairie dropseed   by some contaminant
from the production of TNT   once made

        The water flow red   igloos of ammunition
slice hill & loam   subsurface sandpit wingtip
calamity   purplish red June-grass
             in spring rain   bird from bullet   slave to
discontinuous fields   to chemical works & of seeing

Empire of Grass

A lean-to against a slope   blighted
creek bed   dogs barking in a field
after cut hay   bees swarming
a hollowed tree   two maladies
merged into a single strap of grass

Feel dry stones in my pocket
tiny sounds of gnashing   a coda
ice against loess peaks   hard maple & beech
"deep galleries in the underlying limestone"
remorse in the shape of a square mile

"Capacious heedlessness" he said
a green-winged teal skating on water
spring ferns turning copper   acute death
becomes chronic wallow   we waded
out to the stream's island & stayed

Yellow warblers in the marsh weed
marsh wren in the bulrush   portage
of sand   gaggle of white-fronted geese
salmon-footed   flutter of arm of leg
a boy stuck in a tree   again & again

*

"All flesh is grass"   he said
we've no interest in the past
vines wrapped about our waists
our wrists & ankles   threadless slag
tiptoe through carpentered world

Bedrock house for sun or horse
butterfly   dog   cloud   gnarl of
dark green conifers   against the bricks
a snail slinks in the dark   red-bodied
"ether/acre   wearing a sod gown"

No sharp gradients   only small hillocks
& the two of us   mosquitoes crowding
our dusk-camp   a wolf in the goldstem
elk skull at the crossing   soft lines
of tallgrass in wind   turkey-footed origin

Fox sparrow dips behind the hedge
gray-headed & singing   we woke
to successive layers   we weren't the first
cattail convolution   bird's-foot violet
a half-eaten shrew   lingering as speck & gut

*

Pocket gophers burrow under blue
milk-vetch   relict patches   *star*
in *start* & *stark*   pasqueflower blooms
on glacial moraine   two whale ribs
in the rafters   exiled hemispheres

"Bleak swells" & "our blank
in bliss to fill"   chickadee nest in a snag
crepuscular sphinx moth & its prairie-
white-fringed orchid   tree-shaped
void in the midnight fog

Compass-plant marks the edge
of us &   "granary   smokehouse   root
cellar"   this propensity for limitlessness
within limits   hundreds of great plains toads
hibernating in loose soil until rain

A single Labrador tea plant
found in an Iowa ice-cave in summer
our path through pine barrens
over redroot   "arrow-straight furrows"
meadow mice & open wastes

*

You reach the graveyard before me
old plots filled with big bluestem
"city & wilderness shifting antinomies"
redolent co-minglers   began with
landtheft tinderbox plowshare

Tendency as state of mind like
distil or *filament*   as the heron hunts
a line forms in water   & we say
"have you a brook in your little heart"
a craggy savannah   an inclination for flat & low

Tantamount   leaf-mash   mend-maker
moon grows large under haze
tonight   frog song again   side-oats
& wild indigo   salvage rope & boat
& home   "vault of sky" & whipsaw

A tree swallow in a bluebird's box
wind-break rookery at field's end
the sumac's red wing folded inside
day   a light rain as we hike the broken
road   the ramshackle & outermost

Notes

Voices in conversation throughout these poems are Emily Dickinson, Susan Howe, Thomas Jefferson, Lorine Niedecker, Aldo Leopold, Charles Darwin, Joanna Newsom, and Bon Iver.

Many texts are also in conversation. Richard Manning's *Grassland*, John Manson's *Where the Sky Began*, and numerous field-guides make the once expansive prairie real again. Erik Seeman's *Death in the New World*, Antonius Robben's *Death, Mourning, and Burial*, Nancy Isenberg and Andrew Burstein's *Mortal Remains*, and other volumes illuminate the world of the dead past and present.

On the role of art and literature in the natural world: Leo Marx's *Machine in the Garden*, Elizabeth Willis' *Radical Vernacular: Lorine Niedecker and The Poetics of Place*, Bonnie Costello's *Shifting Ground*, Agnes Denes' *The Human Argument* and Laura Smith's *Wilderness into Civilized Shapes*. And regarding our influence on and interaction with flora and fauna on this continent and others: Mark V. Barrow's *Nature's Ghosts*, Yi-Fu Tuan's *Topophilia*, E. O. Wilson's *Biophilia*, Paul Wapner's *Living into the End of Nature* and Wallace Stegner's *Wolf Willow*.

In "Grass for Bone" the phrase "house of wooden fingers" belongs to Eric Baus. "The dead boy was found clasping a tree" in "Solitary Branches and Small Leaves" is Rae Armantrout's line and "a grave between the rocks," Wellen Smith's.

"Hearts all one stone" in "Star or Plow" is attributed to Wequash, a seventeenth-century Pequot leader. On his deathbed Wequash allegedly said, "me so big naughty heart, me heart all one stone." Roger Williams, theologian and ethnographer, claimed to have converted Wequash to Protestantism.

"Pope County, Illinois" was composed and collaged from Michael J. McNerney's short text *Early Pioneer Gravestones of Pope County, Illinois,* an essay that traces the history and genealogy of folk-carved anthropomorphic headstones in Southern Illinois.

Agnes Denes's project *Rice/Tree/Burial* and Robert Kincaid's *The Wilderness Road,* an outdated depiction of European settlers' journeys west of the Appalachians, converge in "Plum Blossoms at Yellow Dusk." "I have been a long time in this story of land-sigh half-bends and song-crime" is a line of Karla Kelsey's and "to find her trail devoured by birds," Rae Armantrout's.

"Midewin" is a 20,000 acre prairie restoration project located in Northern Illinois.

Acknowledgments

Grateful acknowledgment to the editors at the following journals for publishing poems from this collection:

Beloit Poetry Journal: "Grass for Bone"
Chicago Review: "Taxonomic" and "Pope County, Illinois"
Cincinnati Review: "The Edge Effect"
Free Verse: "Large Stone on Body, Birch Branches Above"
kadar koli: "Solitary Branches & Small Leaves"
The Laurel Review: "Star or Plow"
Salamander: "Grist"
The Sonora Review: "Plum Blossoms at Yellow Dusk"
Thrush: "Broad Wings above Tall Grass"
TYPO: "Simulacra."

Thank you to the Sitka Center for Art and Ecology for an important and beautiful six weeks on the central Oregon Coast. My deepest gratitude to Jon Thompson with Free Verse Editions and David Blakesley at Parlor Press for making this book a reality.

Thanks to my family: my mother, Kathy Zeman; Matt and Jacquie Zeman; and Robin and Steve Read for sharing their passion for all things green and wild in the Midwest. Thank you especially to Susan Tichy, my mentor and friend. And to Eric Pankey, another generous GMU professor. Thank you to Lisa Ampleman, Renee Angle, Jess Anthony, Courtney Campbell, and Danika Myers-Hurwitz for their thoughtful reading of this work before it was finished. And to other friends: Francine Appleton, Jennifer Price, Ann Farrar, Lisa Higgs, John McCarthy, Adam Clay, and companions: Peggy Sue and Ari.

Special thanks to my husband Matt for time and for co-piloting many prairie and birding road trips. And for Lucy, who joined us later.

About the Author

Tracy Zeman's poems have appeared in *Beloit Poetry Journal, Chicago Review, TYPO* and other journals, and her book reviews have been published in *Kenyon Review Online* and *Colorado Review*. She has earned residencies from the Sitka Center for Art and Ecology, Ox-Bow, and The Wild. She lives outside Detroit, Michigan, with her husband and daughter. *Empire* is her first full-length collection.

Photograph of the author by Lai Long. Used by permission.

Free Verse Editions

Edited by Jon Thompson

13 ways of happily by Emily Carr
& in Open, Marvel by Felicia Zamora
Alias by Eric Pankey
At Your Feet (A Teus Pés) by Ana Cristina César, edited by Katrina
 Dodson, translated by Brenda Hillman and Helen Hillman
Bari's Love Song by Kang Eun-Gyo, translated by Chung Eun-Gwi
Between the Twilight and the Sky by Jennie Neighbors
Blood Orbits by Ger Killeen
The Bodies by Christopher Sindt
The Book of Isaac by Aidan Semmens
The Calling by Bruce Bond
Canticle of the Night Path by Jennifer Atkinson
Child in the Road by Cindy Savett
Condominium of the Flesh by Valerio Magrelli, translated by
 Clarissa Botsford
Contrapuntal by Christopher Kondrich
Country Album by James Capozzi
The Curiosities by Brittany Perham
Current by Lisa Fishman
Day In, Day Out by Simon Smith
Dear Reader by Bruce Bond
Dismantling the Angel by Eric Pankey
Divination Machine by F. Daniel Rzicznek
Elsewhere, That Small by Monica Berlin
Empire by Tracy Zeman
Erros by Morgan Lucas Schuldt
Fifteen Seconds without Sorrow by Shim Bo-Seon, translated by Chung
 Eun-Gwi and Brother Anthony of Taizé
The Forever Notes by Ethel Rackin
The Flying House by Dawn-Michelle Baude
Go On by Ethel Rackin
Instances: Selected Poems by Jeongrye Choi, translated by Brenda
 Hillman, Wayne de Fremery, & Jeongrye Choi
The Magnetic Brackets by Jesús Losada, translated by Michael Smith
 & Luis Ingelmo
Man Praying by Donald Platt
A Map of Faring by Peter Riley

The Miraculous Courageous by Josh Booton
Mirrorforms by Peter Kline
No Shape Bends the River So Long by Monica Berlin & Beth Marzoni
Not into the Blossoms and Not into the Air by Elizabeth Jacobson
Overyellow, by Nicolas Pesquès, translated by Cole Swensen
Physis by Nicolas Pesquès, translated by Cole Swensen
Pilgrimage Suites by Derek Gromadzki
Pilgrimly by Siobhán Scarry
Poems from above the Hill & Selected Work by Ashur Etwebi, translated
    by Brenda Hillman & Diallah Haidar
The Prison Poems by Miguel Hernández, translated by Michael Smith
Puppet Wardrobe by Daniel Tiffany
Quarry by Carolyn Guinzio
remanence by Boyer Rickel
Rumor by Elizabeth Robinson
Settlers by F. Daniel Rzicznek
Signs Following by Ger Killeen
Small Sillion by Joshua McKinney
Split the Crow by Sarah Sousa
Spine by Carolyn Guinzio
Spool by Matthew Cooperman
Summoned by Guillevic, translated by Monique Chefdor &
    Stella Harvey
Sunshine Wound by L. S. Klatt
System and Population by Christopher Sindt
These Beautiful Limits by Thomas Lisk
They Who Saw the Deep by Geraldine Monk
The Thinking Eye by Jennifer Atkinson
This History That Just Happened by Hannah Craig
An Unchanging Blue: Selected Poems 1962–1975 by Rolf Dieter
    Brinkmann, translated by Mark Terrill
Under the Quick by Molly Bendall
Verge by Morgan Lucas Schuldt
The Wash by Adam Clay
We'll See by Georges Godeau, translated by Kathleen McGookey
What Stillness Illuminated by Yermiyahu Ahron Taub
Winter Journey [Viaggio d'inverno] by Attilio Bertolucci, translated by
    Nicholas Benson
Wonder Rooms by Allison Funk

www.ingramcontent.com/pod-product-compliance
Lightning Source LLC
LaVergne TN
LVHW041307080426
835510LV00009B/894